Chris Rice

On

Culture:

Small minds, big business, & the psychedelic
solution

ISBN: **1494495155**
ISBN-13: **978-1494495152**

DEDICATION

To my family, for encouraging my inquisitive nature,
My teachers for nurturing it,
My friends for challenging it,
and my love for not finding it *too* ridiculous.

INTRODUCTION

When I began writing out the text that would become "On Culture", I hadn't realized that I was in the early stages of writing a book. Rather, I sought out to jot down my impression of the herb the Mazatec indians of Oaxaca Mexico refer to as the eye of the shepherdess. However, as thoughts often tend to do, mine drifted away from the experience itself to the subjugation of the plant in various states across the globe in recent years, and recent frenzy surrounding this sacred shamanic herb in the never ending newshole that is transmitted to our television sets. How could anything so beautiful be regarded with such contempt and misunderstanding?

I knew this absolutely wasn't the first time that the media

has concocted public outcry. I knew that this wasn't the first time a government did things for their own interests and not the interest of every man either. Lastly, I knew that people all too often fall victim to the mass media hysteria, not realizing that it is all just a ploy to boost ratings and sell advertising space. The objective, for me, became writing a sort of "how to" guide for informing the people who surround you that things are not always as they seem, and that the status quo is not good enough. The result was the following book, "Chris Rice On Culture: Small Minds, Big Business, and the Psychedelic Solution". I hope that this text can help to inform people that we can, indeed, create our own path as a civilization; that you are not helpless, that it is not hopeless, and that *you* elect the government, *you* purchase products from the corporations, and *you,* therefore, are the one with all the power. Without further a due, On Culture.

Chris Rice
January, 2014

ON **CULT**URE

.

CHAPTER 1

I woke from a day dream and found myself in the dry heat of

the desert, staring into the bright mid day sun. As the sun's

brilliance became too much to bare, I diverted my eyes to

the mountains, to the adobo huts. Where was I? The

question seemed like it had already been answered. I felt no

worry, no anguish, an almost deja vu like sense of familiarity.

But I am from New England, I have never left the north east;

how could I experience remembrance of the desert?

I didn't have much time to contemplate it any further, as a band of men in traditional hispanic garb drew near. There appearance was remniscent of farmers in an old John Steinbeck novel. The leader, a middle aged man with a Clint Eastwood disposition approached me. "Are you of *The Andréic Exit?*" He asked in a language I had never heard, even in passing, but that, for some reason, translated easily in my head. What was the right answer? These men had pitchforks, torches, swords, bows, and arrows. It was of the utmost importance that I answered to their liking, but how could I do so when I wasn't even sure what *The Andréic Exit* was? The hardest part was that, because this land appeared so familiar to me, there was a good chance I, indeed, *was* a part of this group of which I had no recollection.

"Yes, I am." I said with confidence.

A smile arose on the man's face. "Bueno."

Chris Mongeau's "Last Frontier" Photographed in the Chisos Mountains in Texas, 2013

He looked at his men, and tilted his head to the left "Viene!" With that, we all followed the man, as he kicked the hind leg of the mule I hadn't even noticed he was on. We were on our way, but to where?

The next thing I knew we were attacking an enormous beast. The beast growled furiously, making the tyrannical roar of Godzilla appear as though it were a cat's meow, but he didn't seem to fight back. Our tiny arrows soared through the dry desert air, but they caused him no real pain. The monster felt refreshed, as though the arrows were a cool, gentle stream of water splashing against his face, replenishing him in the sweltering desert heat.

Wait, what the fuck? How could I tell how the monster *felt*? I noticed, then, that I could see through his eyes now. The pitchforks, the fire, the arrows, it was all happening so fast, but I couldn't see myself there amongst The Andréic Exít, not anymore. I was the monster now.

Just then, the illusion started to slip away, as the arrows continued to fly at my face, I saw that they truly *were* water. There were no townspeople, no Andréic Exít, I was simply splashing myself in the face in the shower of my mom's small town Massachusetts apartment. This was my first experience entering The Kingdom of *Salvia Divinorum*. And that was the most harrowing of it. I had just tried what is arguably one of the most mind altering psychedelic substances known to man, and the worst that happened was me splashing myself in the face with water.

Despite it's timidity, however, Salvia, a member of the mint family, is fast approaching a nationwide prohibition in the United States, similar to the one it has faced in other nations like Russia, Canada, and Ireland, and long term bans on other entheogens such as cannabis, psilocybin mushrooms, and peyote. But this story is not about Salvia Divinorum, it's not even *really* about psychedelics (though I will be focusing on this subject a great deal). It is about civil liberties. It is about social control. It is about the regulation the powers that be have on labor, on cognition, on nearly every facet of life. It is about our duty to help wake up our friends, our neighbors, and our family who are still living in the dream governments the world over have concocted as a way to stay wealthy and powerful while the masses struggle to get by. It is about some of the simple, and often subtle, ways in which we can stop it.

But let's continue where we left off, as psychedelic drugs are something of particular interest. Using psychedelics to "party", the way one would with alcohol, is a serious misuse of these ancient mind expanding tools. Shamans used these healing plants to explore other esoteric planes of existence like heaven and hell. Though the prospect of a bearded man in the sky or an unfathomably terrible place of flames and torture seem about as real as Santa Claus and the Boogey Man, recent developments in the field of cosmological metaphysics make the possibility of these being tangible places rather than simply dogmatic concepts plausible.

CHAPTER 2

As a general rule, most of us common people are not
well versed in the world of physics. Even those of us who are
mildly familiar with the general precepts of say, string theory
or quantum mechanics, would be remiss to say that we
could adequately explain them to others. This is a job best
left to physicists. While I do not purport to know a great deal

about the subject, there are many mind blowing new concepts coming out about our universe or lack thereof. As interesting as all of these innovations are, the two that are of relevance to the present discussion are the prospect of additional dimensions, and the multiverse theory.There are many revered scientists within the field of cosmological physics who believe in some form of multiverse as well as additional dimensions, among them Stephen Hawking, Neil Degrasse Tyson, and Michio Kaku, who are all sort of celebrities in that field. However, exploration of these additional universes or dimensions (or both, whichever the case may be) proves impossible as they are, by nature, outside of our realm of consciousness. We as human beings experience 4 dimensions in the form of length, width, height, and time. This does not mean those are the only 4 dimensions in existence. Instead, it means that the evolutionary constraints of our sensory organs allow for the perception of only 4 dimensions. This is probably because our senses have not yet evolved far enough to perceive these additional dimensions. As J.B.S. Haldane once put it "Not only is the universe stranger than we imagine, it is stranger than we *can* imagine." The idea that our primate brain is capable of understanding every level of a vast, infinitely expanding, and unfathomably complex universe from the microcosm to the macrocosm is truly naïve.

Conversely, it may be that visualizing these additional dimensions may have made our world too difficult to navigate in prehistoric times, and so we evolved to make our brains better suited for navigating the jungles in the hunter-gatherer lifestyle our ancestors sustained on planet earth[i].

You see, every version of string theory has 10 dimensions, with the exception of M-theory (a "universal theory of everything" so to speak) which, while in its infancy, holds that there are 11. Could it be that by opening the floodgates of perception through the use of psychedelic compounds we can somehow access dimensions outside of our ordinary level of perception, almost as if to temporarily stimulate those underutilized sectors of the human brain, and the neuro-chemicals we evolved away from using? It is entirely plausible. But there is, of course, another explanation for these altered states of consciousness.

The multiverse theory states that there are numerous universes (perhaps an infinite number) that operate outside of our universe. The world of cosmological physics is beyond my scope of comprehension, but who is to say that buried within those black holes there isn't a universe working in tandem with our own? In it, another Milky Way galaxy, another solar system, even another earth just like our own, but in this one you took a different life path. Through the next black hole, a universe in which the walls breathe. Through another black hole, an earth in which the place where my mothers apartment sits (in *our* universe) is instead replaced by the desert home of a monstrous Djinn. Psychedelics may allow us to access these universes within a multiverse.

Perhaps they can even explain cryptozoological phenomena like ghosts and shadow people, even aliens, as creatures from other dimensions finding their way into our own. Certainly, this can not presently be proven. But science has little to say about subjective experience, and so it can also not be disproven.

But if that's the case, where do these machine elves, these serpents, these self bouncing jeweled basketballs go when we are not in altered states of consciousness? Does the western perception that they are all products of your imagination, simply hallucinations to be ignored hold true? Or, may it be that there is something to be learned about cosmology, about black holes, dimensional travel, even time travel which we can access by temporarily swapping out the neuro-chemicals in that inefficient machine that is the mammalian brain for those which our ancestors incidentally discovered while roaming through the jungles? We may not find answers to these questions in the darkest reaches of our cerebrum, but we owe it to ourselves, on occasion to illuminate those darkest of places and to see whatever our primate brain *can* perceive.

CHAPTER 3

Regardless of it's ability or inability to allow us access to other universes, other dimensions, the spirit world, or whatever name you may attribute to these different planes of existence, there are some things that we do *absolutely* know about psychedelics.

For starters, psychedelics allow for a deep introspection.

Because these compounds temporarily eliminate what Freud dubbed the ego, we are able to see deep into our own psyche. Through this, many people have come to deep revelations about their own behavior. Psychedelics have been touted as a cure for everything from PTSD to heroin addiction. some claims even go so far as to say that they cease tumor growth in cancer patients, and raise t-cells in AIDS patients (as a result of their stress reducing properties.) Certainly anything with this much potential deserves to at least be examined by the scientific community. However, prohibition of these substances *even in the hands of doctors* prevents such research.

Take for instance autism. A small scale 1963 study[ii] of the effects of psychedelic drugs on autistic, socially inept, and developmentally delayed children showed great potential in these drugs for the treatment of such illnesses. Some of these patients were (as many autistic people are) non-communicative before taking psychedelic drugs, and during the sessions (sometimes even afterwards) showed a beautiful and extensive vocabulary. In addition, children with social ineptitude seemed to come out of their shells, and remained as such once the medication wore off.

It should be noted, though, that within these examples, a majority of the patients had come from abusive backgrounds and, as psychological disorders are considered by many to be as much genetic as they are environmental, it is not entirely certain that this would work for all patients. But then again, I am not a doctor, and even if I was, I couldn't get my hands on psychedelics[iii]. The fact of the matter is, though psychedelic drugs are, at the very least, worthy of scientific inquiry for medicinal use, governments the world over have taken hard line stances against them. So why, exactly, is this the case?

CHAPTER 4

One conceivable reason for the prohibition of

psychedelic studies, even in the care of trained

professionals, is that psychedelic psychotherapy is not

inherently profitable. For instance, The Multidisciplinary

Association for Psychedelic Studies research into the use of

MDMA for the treatment of Post Traumatic Stress Disorder

finds that, in order to effectively treat PTSD the compound would only have to be administered a couple of times...ever.

This is a stark contrast to the various treatments for PTSD that are currently on the market. The majority of these prescriptions need to be taken, at the very least, daily. Critically thinking, the logical solution for a drug company would be to have these individuals take a drug daily for the rest of their lives rather than have treatment administered only a handful of times. In much the same way that heart surgery is more profitable than prevention of heart disease, and treating cancer (and fundraising for a hypothetical future "cure") is more profitable than curing it, the treatment of mental illness, such as PTSD, depression, anxiety, and similar ailments is much more profitable than pouring money into the research of compounds, such as MDMA, that were discovered so long ago that no one has the legal right to patent them. In fact, it would be in their best fiscal interest to do what they can to prevent the legalization, medical or otherwise, of these substances so as to keep the ailing members of our society on a leash.

As a result of the overprescription of pharmaceuticals, our society has seen an increase in prescription drug related deaths as well as widespread addiction to pain medication. In addition, the mentally ill of my generation, with their daily dose of serotonin reuptake inhibitors have become increasingly numb and apathetic. This phenomenon has directly contributed to recent spree killings such as the infamous Newtown Connecticut shooting. The sad reality is, short term profits are more important to the pharmaceutical industry than the long term welfare of our society or the wellbeing of the individuals within it.

Psychedelics are also illegal for their boundary dissolving principals. As Terrence McKenna once put it, "Psychedelics are illegal not because a loving government is concerned that you might jump out of a third story window. Psychedelics are illegal because they dissolve opinion structures and culturally laid down models of behavior and information processing. They open you up to the possibility that everything you know is wrong." People the world over are one or two profound experiences away from self actualization. They are so close to the realization that the world is about more than being the person with the most toys; that this life is *not* a journey whose goal is a destination, but instead a song or a dance to be enjoyed.

But the entire economic structure, moreover, the power structure, of the industrialized world hinges on the fact that you won't come to this realization; so they keep us occupied and happy with our huge flat screen televisions and our fast food and our iPhones and our laptops like the one I am typing on now. And peer pressure makes you want that new iPhone, that Google Glass[iv], because you don't want to be the outcast. And so you go to work so you can afford such things, and when you get them, you realize you really aren't any happier in the long run. You just have more... *stuff*. And that is the illusion of culture.

The fact that you might realize life is about more than that frightens the CEOs, their hands eternally in the back pocket of the government. And the government itself, in its constant desire for tax money and exponential power growth, can't have the possibility that you'll realize the rat race is a fraud. It's too risky for them to allow psychedelics on the market for psychotherapy or otherwise.

But there is a way of familiarizing the masses with the truth surrounding both the baseless dominator culture that we have subjected ourselves to since the dawn of the industrial revolution (more specifically in the past 50 years) and the medicinal and, further, psycho-neuro-immunologically therapeutic effects that psychedelics and even cannabis can have on human beings; mind, body, and soul. What's more, it doesn't cost us any lives, it doesn't take any bloodshed, and it doesn't even necessarily require the consumption of psychedelics by the masses to accomplish (although it certainly wouldn't hurt!) v

CHAPTER 5

The first tool we find in our arsenal is the same one used

by the gay rights movement. The sociological framework that

gay rights advocates constructed for themselves, however

complex it may have become at times, was simply that they

were people, just like everyone else. Until as late as the

1960's, homosexuality was categorized as a mental illness

for which electric shock therapy was the most widely accepted treatment. This was used in an attempt to force the reintroduction and acceptance of societal norms by people who the culture at large considered "sick."

In much the same way, society deems users of psychedelics at best as new age hippie idiots and at worst as drug addicts in need of some variety of intervention; souls lost to chemical dependence (an ironic notion, considering psychedelic compounds, especially those occurring in nature, do not carry the addictive properties found in most scheduled substances or even *unscheduled* ones such as tobacco, alcohol, caffeine or even wheat.)

You see, we have all been culturally conditioned to believe in the propaganda that is fed to us by the mass media[vi]. For instance, yesterday I turned on a popular morning news broadcast only to see the headline, "Things your hair dresser won't tell you." Meanwhile, there are entire countries stricken with poverty, illness, and famine, our government has autonomous weaponry, such as drones, with a stunningly low accuracy (resulting in an estimated 98% civilian casualty rate) and lobbyists from the world's largest corporations finance political campaigns, thus ensuring the law regarding their particular industry is written to protect said industry, not the electorate. Suffice to say, this information does not permeate the bubble in which the general populous lives. One must seek out information in order to obtain it, and even then finding a credible, legitimate, and objective source is an arduous task in and of itself.

Relating this back to cannabis and other entheogens, the party line has always been that these substances are problematic, causing their users to lose brain cells, commit crimes, transition to narcotics, or otherwise behave unfavorably. In reality, the majority of the problems associated with entheogens are due to their prohibition, and the fact that they are lumped into the blanket category of "drugs" simply shows a serious misunderstanding and lack of knowledge on these age old tools.

But to come out in support of something like psychedelics or campaign finance reform in a world caught up in the daily lives of the Kardashians or superfluous "news" casts like the one mentioned above puts you in the undesirable category of marginalized intellectual. And, as our cultural programming has instilled in our minds, the braniac is a strange, friendless and sexless creature to be avoided at all costs. Would they portray it any other way?

In the case of homosexuality, the gay rights movement was able to break free from the stagnated societal views associated with their subculture in a generally peaceable and matter of fact way: They came out. It is much harder to hate homosexuals when you realize your son, your brother, your next door neighbor, your coworker or your best friend is gay. As homosexuals poured out of the closets and into the streets, they found acceptance by a society with the propensity for xenophobia. But Rome wasn't built in a day. It was a long, slow moving process from the Stonewall riots to Queer Eye for the Straight Guy. And even as this is being written, the fight is still not over, with gay marriage only legal in a handful of states.

If psychedelic users (and cannabis users alike) employed this same tactic of coming out, the world would recognize them for what they are. Not simply hippies or drug addicts or fools. Intelligent, articulate people from all walks of life such as lawyers, psychologists, scientists and engineers; your brother, your neighbor, your son. We're here, we're weird, get used to it.

But parallels with the gay rights movement can only take us so far. Certainly, not everyone is in a position that allows them to tell their friends, family, or especially coworkers that they have tripped on magic mushrooms. For some people, such as school teachers, this could be a career ender. But that is *right now.*

That's why it's so important for those of us who are able to come out to do so. By opening up the public discourse on psychedelics, we are breaking ground for those people in hopes of creating a dialogue, so that they may be able come out in the near future. In acknowledging that good, honest people within their own lives have broken through to the other side without any negative repercussions, people one by one the world over may soon realize that arguments in favor of psychedelics are not simply a pastiche of the 1960s counterculture. Rather, they are legitimate claims in favor of substances that help human beings realize there is more to life than our egos, in conjunction with culture, allow us to perceive.

CHAPTER 6

But coming out isn't the only apparatus available to us in
swaying the public opinion on whether or not a human being
is allowed to explore their own consciousness. There is a
radical, new tool available to us that, despite being in it's
infancy, is already changing the way the world works. So
much so, in fact, that both The U.K. And the U.S. Are

contemplating resolutions to severely limit its usage while

other countries have already began to do so. This device,

which is not only beginning to enlighten the masses about

the truth behind psychedelics, but also garner support for the

movement against our irresponsible and non-responsive

culture, is called the internet. [vii]

The internet is something that every last one of us is

familiar with, but it snuck up on us in such a way that most

people don't quite fully understand the gravity of the

situation. Unbeknownst to most people, the internet has

existed in some form or another for over 40 years, since the

United States government developed ARPANET. The 1990s

saw the dawn of the world wide web, which lay almost in a

stage of dormancy until the new millennium. Then, with the

advent of high speed internet in cohesion with increasingly

fast processing speed, the internet was suddenly

everywhere. We often don't think about this, but Facebook,

YouTube, Twitter, and smartphones like the iPhone and

Google's Android are all under 10 years old, and have only been a part of the average American's lives for under 5 years. Despite this staggering fact, we can hardly imagine a world without a communicator in our pocket with which we can send a message, a picture, or even a video across the world in under a minute, or a time when all the facts that there are to be known weren't easily available to us through a quick Google search. And this is just the beginning. These terms in and of themselves would have made literally no sense to many people of the early 2000s, and now they are household names. With the rapid succession of technological advancements snowballing exponentially, it is inconceivable to imagine what lies 30, 20, or even 10 years in our future.

However, the first wave of societal effects that these technological advancements have created are already being felt. They have taken the shape of political protests and the ousting of long established regimes. Perhaps the earliest example of this occurred just over 3 years ago in the form of the Arab Spring. What began as the overthrow of totalitarian governments across the Middle East in favor of democratic election has, in some instances throughout the Arab world, given way to far right Islamofascism. In the most famous case of this, Egyptian protestors dethroned President Hosni Mubarak eventually replacing him with Mohamed Morsi. Morsi shortly thereafter declared himself immune from legal challenge, in effect making himself supreme leader of Egypt and was himself ousted in a coup d'etat.

Regardless of the unfavorable outcome, the protestors in both of these circumstances as well as similar events in Libya, and other nations organized through the use of a powerful strategic tool in social networking. Gone are the days when dissenters struggled to find like minded individuals among their immediate surroundings. The internet has replaced the quiet, fearful words of the oppressed with demands for equality through the use of sites like Twitter, and widespread international support.

The Syrian Civil War saw the dejected citizens of Syria using these same tools to fight their own draconian government. The world at large turned a blind eye to the miserable conditions of the Syrian people until evidence was released that chemical weapons were used against Syrian rebels.[viii] Because multimedia no longer needs to go through the traditional channels of nervous, state funded news organizations, and also in part because of the hyperavailability of recording technology (i.e. smart phones) this video evidence was broadcast the world over within an amount of time that would have been unimaginable even 5 years ago.

And the serious power that this tool provides to a formerly voiceless people isn't entirely lost on the west, either. Here in the United States, the war machine began rolling, as it all too often does. President Obama and (our former anti-war activist turned Secretary of State) John Kerry were trying to fuel American support for US involvement in the Syrian Civil War. All of this came to a screeching halt when American citizens, frustrated with an ever compounding national debt, and tired of being the world's police, took to the internet to voice their disdain. Suddenly, Obama and Russia's Prime Minister Putin (one of Syria's greatest supporters) came to a peaceable agreement. Though we cannot be entirely sure what role a lack of public support had in these negotiations, one might note that the last time a president began beating the drum of war there was no alternative news source, no rapidly transmitted meme of contempt. Rather, there by the president's side were the dinosaurs that are traditional media, beating the drums of war in unison, as their corporate sponsors undoubtedly demanded of them. Rat-tat. Rat-tat.

Another instance of the internet's power to transform public opinion exists in the Occupy movement, which sought to disrupt an unconscionable wealth disparity by throwing a cog into the insatiable machine that is capitalism. Their protests were organized largely on the internet with widespread support coming from people all over the world. Unfortunately with a lack of organization, structure, or clearly stated goals, and with government shills purporting to be protestors causing violence at Occupy events[ix], the movement quickly lost steam.[x]

CHAPTER 7

Now, imagine if Occupy, whose ideology was at least

admirable, *did* have structure and *did* have a clear set of

goals. What might have been accomplished? Imagine if

Gandhi, or Martin Luther King had the tools of the internet

and social media available to them. I strongly doubt they'd

be looking at Cats That Look Like Hitler or playing Candy Crush. Rather, they would be doing the same things that made them so great; they would be forcing information through the bubble to a society who does not outwardly seek that information and thusly doesn't acquire it. They would be making people who *deserve* to feel uncomfortable for their unconscionable and outdated views feel fearful that their abhorrent social constructs may soon fall by the wayside. The difference? With the internet, these men's jobs would have been made significantly easier. The rapid transferral of information from common man to common man may be in its early stages, but, as you can see, it *will be* the most important world-changing invention since Gutenberg started the Printing Revolution.

So I implore you, you psychedelic thinkers, you marginalized intellectuals, you who are fed up with a system that was not built for you, but instead built for money making entities and the elite who preside over them, built to enforce a power structure that prevents inquiry in fear of liberty to stand up for your convictions. It may feel like an uphill battle, and in many ways it is, but the flow of information is faster than ever and while you may feel, at times, like an ant facing an army of tanks, remember that the ratio is 99:1; the odds are heavily in *our* favor.

This is not meant to incite a riot, as militias are stupendously pedestrian. The United States not only has the worlds largest military,[xi] but their arsenal now includes both autonomous weaponry as well as various nuclear bombs. To suppose that a farmer, or even a legion of farmers, with AK47s or what have you could disassemble the world's largest superpower is a romantic notion (I suppose) but completely anti-intellectual. These organizations are tremendously defensive of their right to bear arms, meanwhile the government has quietly stripped away many other rights through the patriot act, related NSA spying, NDAA, and an authorization of drone use on American citizens without a trial. The NRA didn't so much as bat an eyelid at any of these intrusions into civilian life, at least not publically. In this way, the issue of guns is merely a distraction[xii].

Instead, the idea is to capture the fervor of the Occupy Movement, and channel it in such a way as to achieve goals on both a socio-economic and geopolitical scale. The idea is to sell peace, love, and human compassion as a product that *everyone* will enjoy, if only they see it as ascertainable. The idea is that, through social media, we can accomplish this in as little as one generation by forcing it through the bubble the same way MLK, and Gandhi did, and the same way Coca Cola and Kay's Jewelers and Toyota force their advertisements through the bubble now.

It is no exaggeration that, through the means of communication presently available to us, we can make the counterculture of the 1960s appear paltry in comparison to what our generation is capable of. But, certainly, we won't be able to change everyone's minds. If human beings are one thing, it is resistant to change. But while many people are steadfast in their beliefs, it takes just a few to get the snowball rolling so that the moral zeitgeist can evolve, as it did on the civil rights movement, as it did on gay marriage, and as it did in Syria and Egypt. In this, we can make the moral landscape of our future one of love, understanding and camaraderie as opposed to one of partisanship, xenophobia, and greed.

This is the psychedelic solution, but the greater question at hand is, "How do we get there?"

Why is it that government contractors can make money rebuilding Iraq, but not Detroit? Why is it that oil production can be a billion dollar industry and something with a smaller ecological impact, such as solar panels or wind power is ridiculed? Why do we, in America, allow ingredients that are banned throughout the rest of the civilized world into our products, even our food?

These are difficult problems that must be addressed by society, but their solutions are entangled in politics and, at times, difficult to answer. [xiii]Now that the very basic toolset has been identified, the following chapters will demonstrate ways of changing these unadmirable aspects of civilization, for the greater good of society and, furthermore, the planet on which we live.

CHAPTER 8

In the past 100 years, something very interesting has been brewing in American culture. Our natural resources of clean air, water, and food have been slowly eroded. Meanwhile, our civil liberties have been chipped away under the guise of national security, and our lower and middle classes' wealth has been, paradoxically, redistributed into the pockets of the richest one percent of our once great nation.

In exchange, we have continued to buy the goods and services of our nation's richest corporations, we repeatedly elect the same seedy politicians to rule over us term after term, and have become even more productive in the process; in effect, becoming subservient[xiv].

However, due largely in part to both the neo-psychedelic movement and the internet, more and more people each day are waking up to the fact that all of it is a mirage put in place to keep the wealthy in power and the serfs In check. This is where most people leave off. They get the inkling that this is not how it is all supposed to be, but they conclude that the power struggle cannot be won, reluctantly accept their own fate and, though disillusioned, continue on with the the day to day routine as any good worker bee would. But there is another step in the process that seems to have been forgotten. The logical next step in the evolution of thought is to correct the problem through the planning and implementation of change.

Some of the changes society must address in order to continue on appear complicated and arduous. Understandably, not everyone will be willing to participate in the early stages of this societal evolution but the reality is, this paradigm shift is necessary not only for the advancement of the human species, but the survival of our planet as a whole.

If we were to look at our culture objectively from a third person point of view (as psychedelics and other consciousness changing agents allow through their ego-dissolving properties) we would see a shortsighted species throwing an ecological temper tantrum, acting in their own best interest with little regard to the wants, needs, and desires of the other creatures living on our planet, or what our descendents will want a century from now. This short sightedness, caused both by big business as well as a miseducated and disenfranchised society, will undoubtedly be the downfall of our species if we do not make a conscientious effort to stop it.

Our reluctance to change stems from a cultural conditioning perpetuated by world leaders who allow a system to take place in which 1% of the population are enabled to control 40% of the world's entire wealth, while over 30,000 children die of starvation every day. Once this conditioning is broken (through psychedelics, through the internet, through coming out in support of what I have referred to as a psychedelic society, and by extension, a full scale cultural reform) the industrialized world can take steps away from the current socio-economic paradigm and move in the direction of a world where starvation, aristocracy, and environmental desolation are all just unbelievable pieces of our world's barbaric history, as past discriminatory practices like genocide and slavery are considered today.

CHAPTER 9

For the sake of coherence, let's explore this topic in greater detail. There are various facets of society that we accept as just being part of "the way the world works" when, upon further examination, they are counterintuitive to the greater good. Take, for example, the federal reserve system.

Despite it's name, The Federal Reserve is not officially a government organization, but rather a centralized bank chartered by the world's richest men in 1907 as a way to control the flow of money. Since its inception, the value of a dollar has gone down 96%. What's worse, each dollar produced is loaned to the United States Government at interest. Because every dollar ever produced accrues this interest automatically, our government has no choice but to continually borrow more money. In this, our federal tax dollars go towards these interest rates before they ever go towards social programs, thus creating a perpetual system in which more money is borrowed exponentially[xv], in effect, making our government and ourselves **slaves** to the dollar, and by extension, slaves to the bankers.

It's safe to say that none of us were born in 1907, but even if we were, the bill that chartered The Federal Reserve system was pushed through by businessmen and bureaucrats with very little public knowledge and non existent public debate.

In this way, it slipped under the radar of public consciousness and into the law books without ever being voted on by the public [xvi] at large as is the case all too often to this day. This is a particularly diabolical and cruel-intentioned example of something that was precipitated by the ruling class long ago which our society simply continues to accept.[xvii] There are many other instances that are, instead of intentionally malicious, simply antiquated. They are based on outdated science and faulty logic, and were implemented in a time with drastically fewer industrialized nations, and less than half the population density of present day. (Without getting into great detail, a wonderful example of this is the use of fossil fuels.) Further still, there are more contemporary decisions that have been handed down from on high, allegedly for the benefit of mankind, that are an attempt at keeping up with present day population density, the needs of emerging industrialized nations, and the like. A wonderful example of this is genetically modified foods. The idea of modifying organisms so as to create more frost-hardy, insect resistant plants that produce a higher yield of edible material within a particular amount of space seems, at first glance, as though it would be the solution to world hunger. The problem lies in the fact that genetic modification, and pesticides like Monsanto's round-up that coincide with said GMOs, have been shown in some studies to cause tumor growth[xviii],as well as in the realization that Monsanto has taken legal action against farmers who have been using these copy written (you read that right) seeds without their permission[xix]. The problem lies, not only in the fact that this major corporation is trying to monopolize the production of food, but in the fact that congressmen on Monsanto's payroll tried to slip an act through, hidden in the pages of a larger bill, that would prevent judicial review of modified foods[xx] and, even if they had been taken to trial, one of Monsanto's former attorneys is Supreme Court Justice Clarence Thomas (talk about a conflict of interest!). Moreover, the problem lies in the idea that industries like Monsanto perpetuate disinformation by using their astronomical economic influence to censor scientific studies

whose results disagree with the results of said company's

own science and that, despite what any daring scientist may

say against genetically modified crops, no laws will be

passed forcing the labeling of GMOs at a federal level as

long as Monsanto's former vice president, Michael Taylor, is

the head of the Food and Drug Administration[xxi].

CHAPTER 10

As you're probably starting to see, the idea that we have a

democracy by, of, and for the people is just another lovely

fairy tale we are taught in public schools. And that's just a

minor look at the belly of the beast.

The fact of the matter, in all of these instances, is that

scrutiny and public discourse cannot exist in the vacuous

vacuum known as civil obedience. Once we have removed the subjective perception of culture, instead acknowledging that changing these injustices, and questioning these entirely alarming aspects of our society objectively is imperative to our survival as a species, we see that implementing change is crucial to the advancement of human liberties and to the erosion of our corporatocracy in favor of a user-friendly governing system like, say, a legitimate democracy, not unlike the one enacted all those years ago by the enlightenment philosophers we have come to know as our "founding fathers".[xxii]

But all in all, what we're working with is just a system that we have inherited, set in place by people who could not have possibly foreseen suitcase nukes, the internet, or corporations. And like all other systems, it needs to be updated. You don't see people throwing Windows 8 in a 20 year old computer, do you?[xxiii] Our present government is the political equivalent to a silent movie. The government should be thought of as a tool we have developed to make honest decisions in the interest of the people, and not as a domineering, faceless entity which a ruling class can hide behind while slowly enslaving the American public.

You see, the democratic framework still exists in America and we *can* hold the corporate aristocracy accountable for actions we deem detrimental to our society by hitting them where it hurts, in their influence and in their affluence.

It's understandable to feel helpless in all of this, especially with all of the daunting information provided in chapter 9. It can feel like an uphill battle at times, like there's no chance of your horse winning the race, so you might as well rip up your ticket and go home. But the reality is, the race is still neck and neck.

CHAPTER 11

The architecture of our country may have been patched over

by colluding forces with arbitrary laws, hidden bills, and,

increasingly, partisanship for the sake of partisanship, but, buried somewhere in all of that nonsense, the conceptual framework of a great nation is still structurally sound. Our constitution protects very basic, inalienable rights and freedoms of men, not corporations. Politicians, as elected officials, are entrusted with the task of making sure those freedoms are met. I can unequivocally say that this is not the case.

We have all been indoctrinated within our school systems to know that our nation's independence was founded on the principals of life, liberty, and the pursuit of happiness. Because we have been hearing these words for virtually our entire lives, they sometimes fail to convey the meaning which they once carried. Life and the pursuit of happiness are both pretty unambiguous terms, but what about liberty? We all have a vague understanding of what liberty is, but to put things in perspective, here is a dictionary definition of the term:

"Liberty (n.) - the state of being free within society from oppressive restrictions

imposed by authority on one's way of life, behavior, or political views"

If this book has done nothing else so far, it has, at the very least, demonstrated that the idea of the United States government protecting this or either of our other aforementioned rights is nothing other than a part of our nationalistic mythos. But these public servants are supposed to be just that: public servants; and iff they are not serving the public, but instead serving the interest of corporations, then it is time that we elect new public servants.

It's really that simple. There is no need to eradicate the government, there is no need to start militia groups, there is no need for an Oklahoma City Bombing, or fruitless political bickering, which seem to be nothing more than theatrics. We can make society-altering changed within the confines of the system that was put in place by our well-intentioned founding fathers that has since been tainted by snakes in suits. If we just hold these politicians and corporations alike accountable for their actions we can right the wrongs that have been written into our political code.

In the case of politicians, have you ever noticed that the same dubious characters get elected time and time again, and, each time, continue to deliver more of the same? The logical solution is to stop voting for them, and, instead, put someone into office who espouses the same worldview that you do. Whether consciously or not, too many people adhere to Timothy Leary's old adage "Tune In. Turn On. Drop Out."[xxiv] especially in regards to politics. I would, of course, argue in favor of tuning in and turning on, but dropping out is a different story. By self-segregation, you are doing nothing to advance social, cultural, or cognitive liberties. Instead, you are allowing those scoundrels who would never *dream* of dropping out to run the whole show, and, as a result, they've written the laws in such a way that they can monitor your every virtual move on the internet, your every movement through your phone's GPS all while allowing poison to remain legal as entheogens remain an arrestable offense.

This vestige of Leary's counterculture hasn't allowed progress, if anything it has worked against it.

But in order to make the votes count, we cannot allow the two headed monster of our bipartisan system, with their seemingly unlimited wealth, dominate the dialogue. Through the internet, we have a tool with which to throw one of our own into the race, and that is called crowd sourcing.

For those of you who are unaware of the term, crowd sourcing uses websites like IndieGoGo and Kickstarter to allow people to fundraise towards common goals, usually in the production of goods or media, or the building of concert venues, etc. It is absolutely conceivable, though, to develop a crowdsourcing website which allows for the creation of a political campaign (in fact, I have heard talks of activist entrepreneurs working on this very task). We can easily find true representatives of the 99%, with values in line with our own, who do not subscribe to the infantile bickering of the bipartisan system.[xxv] With overwhelming support through social media platforms, the hypothetical candidate (or candidates) would not simply be a wasted vote, as our third party contenders often are, and this is largely due to funding. With the proper funding, said candidate could make those same appearances that the democrats and republicans make. This candidate could pay for television commercials[xxvi] , they could do all of the things that a political candidate does. There are presently well over 300 million people in the United States. If less than half of them gave a dollar to the campaign, it could be a success. Best of all, the candidates allegiance would not be with Big Agro, or Big Oil, or any of the other lobbying groups. Their allegiance would be with the public. A politician by the people, and for the people, bringing the age old concept to fruition once again. If we can do this enough times, we can cure the cancer that has seemingly engulfed our political system and replace it with an equitable system that, at the very least, provides liberty and justice for all.

This active participation in the political process could just as easily be transposed into our purchasing habits as well. As you are undoubtedly aware, corporations number one goal is to make money[xxvii]. For many, it does not matter how this is achieved, but instead simply *that* it is achieved. So when corporations start to lose money because their product is not compliant with the ideals of the public, they begin to take notice.

The elimination of high fructose corn syrup in many foods is exemplary of this. Concerned mothers and those men and women knowledgable on matters of food decidedly stopped purchasing products that included high fructose corn syrup. The corn syrup lobby[xxviii] payed an astronomical amount of money to combat claims of its health hazards through a media campaign that treated the general public as though they were ignoramuses. Ultimately, David beat Goliath, and while there is no ban on this dastardly sugar substitute in sight, many corporations are switching the formula of their products to reclaim their lost market shares.[xxix]

The same can be done with virtually all products, food related or otherwise. Assuming there is a qualitative issue with a product, buy a comparable product that meets your standards. There is no one telling you that you *have* to buy McDonald's or that you *need* to buy your oil from BP. Certainly, avoiding certain conglomerates is more difficult than others, but, ultimately, your boycotting of their goods and services will lead to the improvement of their goods and services or the bankruptcy of their corporation. In either case, this results in the availability of a superior product and is in the best interest of the consumer.

Similarly, if you are involved in the stock market, only invest in things that you *actually* believe in, not necessarily the things that will be the most profitable to you. In doing so, the corporations who are hindering society will have to change their evil ways while the progressive business model will flourish. I, for instance, have invested in, and bare witness to the proliferation of a solar panel company, an organic foods company, and an electric car company, all of which are both beneficial for society and the accumulation of profits.

In some instances, you can even take things a step further, if you are in a position to do so. Purchase your furniture from a local carpenter, not from Pier 1 Imports or Crate & Barrel. Do your banking at a credit union or a small localized bank, not Bank of America, not City Bank.[xxx] You can even take certain matters entirely into your own hands. For instance, starting a community garden which will not only provide you with nearly free food, but will also foster a sense of community between yourself and your neighbors.In addition, it will provide a better use of your time than watching Two and a Half Men reruns interlaced with commercials for furniture stores.

This highjacking of the concepts of social Darwinism works in the favor of every man, woman, and children instead of the profiteering of human misery that these detrimental businesses have caused in our society.

Again, remember, we are the majority. These politicians, these conglomerates only got to their positions of power because we have allowed them to do so. We, the people, have much more power than we often realize. We have the power to stop the madness that surrounds us, but it just takes action.

We have the power to reject the cult of culture and all of the oppression that it stands for through the diagnoses of these societal ills, education of our peers, planning solutions to these problems, and then, ultimately, implementation of these ideals. This is true of psychedelics, this is true of politics, of big business, and of our planet as a whole through the embracing of our custodial relationship with the environment. But if we, the marginalized intellectuals do not act on these instincts, we do not have the right to complain about the state of the world. It is our absolute duty to unite in making the changes we want to see in the world, because,

after all, *"society"* is more than just a word. *We* are the

society, and *we* are responsible for guiding the course of our

future. This world is ours, and it's time to reclaim it while

there is still time to do so!

---

i   . Without getting overly scientific, the structural similarity of
the neurotransmitter serotonin (which, chemically, is 5 hydroxy-
tryptamine) and the psychedelic compound dimethyl*tryptamine,*
which is also endogenous, suggests that the former may very well
have evolved from the latter to allow for an easier navigation of a
4 dimensional world.

ii   The article in question, "The Use of *Psychedelic* Agents with
Autistic Schizophrenic *Children'"* was originally published in
"The Psychedelic Review" and is now free to read online
through various sources.

iii   . Dr. Rick Doblin and his group, MAPS have had some success
in persuading the FDA to approve limited trials of some of these
drugs, especially MDMA, for the first time. Curiously, marijuana is
absolutely off limits for research.

iv This isn't exactly pertinent to this part of the story, but it is
an interesting fact: Because of our cyclical economy,
products are created which are planned to be obsolete
within a short while. This, amongst other things, ensures
that we will purchase the next version of a product, driving
stock prices ever higher. One might attribute all of this to

human nature, but by looking, in contrast, towards egalitarian societies, it's arguable that this is, instead, a matter of cultural programming.

v Now seems as good a time as any to make something perfectly clear, this book speaks a lot about a "psychedelic mind." This does not necessarily refer to a mind on psychedelic substances, or even the mind of a user of psychedelics. Contrarily, many casual users of psychedelics are along for the ride and never obtain "the message". The reality is, there are many ways of accomplishing a form of self-enlightenment (a number of which can be read about in Aldous Huxley's "The Doors of Perception"). The "psychedelic state of mind" I am referring to throughout is one that questions the current state of the world, while embracing our natural place in the ecosystem. People of this disposition believe in the rights and equality of their fellow man, and the human role of stewardship of our planet. In this way, the psychedelic counterculture of the 1960s was on the right track, and psychedelics became illegal in a sweeping 1970 prohibition as a consequence of the potential effect this could have had on societal norms.

vi   . I realize that this may sound like the ranting of a conspiracy theorist, but, objectively, there is a huge gap between UFOlogy or Bigfoot and the prospect that big business and our government both have a say in what is broadcast to our television sets.

vii "The Internet" is a somewhat broad term, almost like "sports" or "music". There are various tools available for the spread of information on the internet. Among them Twitter, Facebook,

Youtube, PDFs/Ebooks, etc. It's up to you to pick which flavor of the internet you most prefer for purveying your views to others. If you believe in a particular cause but find it difficult expressing yourself through the various available media, there is always the sharing of information. Information can spread virally throughout the culture, referred to as "memes". I won't go into great detail on "memes" here, but check out the definitive text on the subject, Richard Dawkins' "The Selfish Gene"

viii It's ironic to me that chemical weapons are where we draw the line. It's as if to say "Bombing, Shooting, stabbing and otherwise killing your own people is fine. What's that? You're using Chemical warfare, so that the amount of time it takes for them to be obliterated is somewhat longer and more drawn out? That's it. We're going after you."

ix This is an interesting fact that very few people know. Police planted "protestors". These agent provocateurs, who were themselves actually police officers, then sought to incite violence at occupy events, causing legitimate protestors to be arrested. In some cases, the violence caused a ripple effect, but in other cases the police officer ended up acting alone. These officers often wore Guy Fawkes masks or other masks so as to disguise the fact that they were indeed cops (there's always the chance they would be recognized). Local officials used these "violent protestors" as a reason to shut down occupy protests, deflating the growing social movement before it was ever able to really take off.

x One could argue, though, that the Occupy Movement is not over. For instance, with the wealth that they acquired in donations, occupy bought up a large amount of debt by people who were crippled by a flailing economy which only advanced the wealth of the rich. It is my personal belief that we have not seen the last of Occupy, in some manifestation or another.

xi America's military is larger than the next 10 nation's armed forces combined.

xii This is not to say the gun debate is without merit. Certainly, there are pros and cons to gun ownership, gun regulation and so forth on a level of personal protection against common criminals, etc. That said, to think that guns could protect you from a motivated government in this day and age is absurd.

xiii What is incontrovertible, however, are the sordid origins of these and other recent cultural constructs.

xiv As Douglas Adams, author of "A Hitchhiker's Guide to The Galaxy" once put it, *"It is a well-known fact that those people who must want to rule people are, ipso facto, those least suited to do it... anyone who is capable of getting themselves made President should on no account be allowed to do the job."* Further research into this phenomena has been done by Dr. Robert Hare, a psychologist who determined that many high ranking CEOs and public officials display characteristics of psychopaths. It is these cold, calculated, cut throat tendencies that have allowed such men and women to climb to the highest rungs of the social and economic latter.

xv   In order to pay for both interest and social programs

xvi   To Make matters worse, it was voted on 2 days before Christmas by a small group of representatives who were backed by the big banks. They did this because they knew that many of the more reputable politicians were already on their way home for christmas (airplanes were not a common way of traveling in the early 1900s). Similar practices have been used by the federal government on other occasions, such as Anslinger's relabeling of cannabis as "marijuana" to prevent senators from knowing what it was they were truly voting to prohibit.

xvii   While I personally am in favor of a resource-based economy, I do not expect a world super-power to upend it's monetary system over night. However, there are equally complex, and equally pressing issues that deserve as much, if not more, of our attention. Some of these issues have to do with our environment, some with our monetary system, some with cognitive and civil liberties, and some with social control. There are too many pressing issues facing us at present time for me to effectively cover all of them here. In addition, I am not a sociological savant and, thus, would not necessarily do justice to certain concepts or theories.

xviii   Let's not even get into the long term environmental impact of pesticides!

xix   This often occurs through accidental cross-pollination from nearby fields.

xx   The Monsanto Protection Act, section 735 of The Consolidated and Further Continuing Appropriations Act, 2013 passed in both the White House and congress, but, fortunately enough for humanity, died in the senate.

xxi This revolving door political schema is not uncommon in our corporatocracy, with regulatory bodies working for the very industries they are supposed to regulate either before or after their time in office. It's difficult to believe that these regulatory bodies are not influenced, then, by these corporations, as high level corporate jobs pay significantly more than the wages seen by most government officials. Outright bribery may be illegal, but, for whatever reason, this revolving door continues to swing perpetually.

xxii   Certainly, there is the issue of the electoral college, but this only poses a problem in presidential elections. I, for one, subscribe to the belief that the electoral college was put in place due to a lack of voter education in the 1770s. No one had television, radio, or even morse code, so the transfer of information was unfathomably slow. The education system was considered far less important than hard labor on farms and religious dogma, and so the founding fathers didn't want the common man spoiling their presidential elections (I can't say that I blame them.) But now with the rapid transfer of information, I believe that it may be time for the electoral college to go by the wayside. The popular vote should count, as it does in state, congressional, and senatorial elections. In addition, it is undoubtedly much harder to buy an entire state than it is to buy individuals within the electoral college. While the electoral college usually votes in the same way that the nation at large does, there are a few examples in our country's history in which there is a discrepancy in the results of the two. The most recent example of this would be the Bush V. Gore election of 2000.

xxiii   There's probably a YouTube video out there somewhere but... come on!

xxiv   Before I get any angry letters, let it be known that Timothy Leary is one of my heroes and without him, I almost certainly would never have started writing this book. That said, "Tune in, Turn on, Drop out" may have been a proper message for the countercultural revolution of the 1960s (mostly because "dropping out" can be seen as a call to non participation in the Vietnam War, but also because society was altogether not prepared for the a psychedelic society. I believe that, with nearly 50 additional years behind us, and educational, unifying tools at our disposal, the majority of people are ready for this cultural renaissance.

xxv   Ross Perot may be an early example of the type of candidate to which I am referring. But while I am proposing crowdsourcing, Perot was just disgustingly rich and threw a cog into the bifurcated machine known as our two party political system entirely on his own. Long before social media was readily available, he took out, for lack of a better word, ad space on broadcast television and made an enormous dent in politics of the 1990s.

xxvi "But why would you?" I asked myself this exact question when writing this portion of the book. But, while many of us live in the future, there are still people who get the bulk of their information from the traditional media sources, however artificial "the news" may seem to many of us.

xxvii There are, of course, exceptions, to this rule. The conscious business movement subscribes to the theory of corporate social responsibility as beneficial to society and the environment, as well as their businesses. We will explore this concept a little as the book moves forward.

xxviii   Known as the Corn Refiner's Association

xxix But beware! The Corn Refiner's Association is privy to the idea that High Fructose Corn Syrup is becoming increasingly unpopular. As a result, they have come up with various other names, like corn sugar, to refer to the product formerly known as High Fructose Corn Syrup. A quick internet search will guide you through the various pseudonyms associated with this chemical.

xxx Visit moveyourmoneyproject.org for more information on switching to local banks and credit unions.

ABOUT THE AUTHOR

Chris Rice is an herbalist from Massachusetts. He is the host of the "Awake with Chris Rice" podcast and has served as a contributing writer for Break Studios and Yahoo's Associated Content. He is the producer of countless songs and short films. He is currently working on a novel entitled "Simulacrum". "On Culture" is his debut book.